Original title:
The Hidden Forest

Copyright © 2024 Creative Arts Management OÜ
All rights reserved.

Author: Aidan Marlowe
ISBN HARDBACK: 978-9916-90-774-0
ISBN PAPERBACK: 978-9916-90-775-7

Echoing Hearts of the Wilderness

In the wild where whispers roam,
The trees stand tall, a verdant home.
Birds take flight on wings of grace,
In nature's arms, we find our place.

Mountains echo with the breeze,
Swaying softly, ancient trees.
Rivers sing a soothing song,
In this realm, we all belong.

A Journey into Verdant Depths

Step by step through emerald trails,
Where sunlight peeks and life prevails.
Every leaf a story told,
In shades of green and glimmers gold.

Mossy beds, a plush embrace,
Nature's peace, a sacred space.
In the depths where shadows play,
We wander forth, come what may.

Luminescence Beneath the Canopy

Beneath the boughs, where light is rare,
Glowing fungi, nature's flair.
Dancing fires in the night,
Stars reflected, pure delight.

Crickets chirp a gentle tune,
Underneath the watchful moon.
Softly glows the world around,
In this magic, peace is found.

Cradled in Nature's Solitude

In quiet nooks where time stands still,
The heart finds comfort, whispers fill.
Gentle breezes stroke the skin,
In solitude, we breathe within.

Each moment holds a lasting peace,
From life's chaos, we find release.
In nature's grasp, our spirits soar,
Cradled softly, forevermore.

A Haven in Nature's Embrace

In the grove where the wildflowers bloom,
A gentle breeze sings a sweet tune.
The trees stand tall, a protective wall,
Nature's whispers echo through all.

Sunlight dances on the forest floor,
Each step reveals what we adore.
A hidden stream plays its soft part,
Inviting peace to every heart.

Patterns of Sun and Shade

Leaves flutter like pages in the light,
Casting shadows that shift in sight.
The sun winks through the branches high,
A patchwork quilt in the evening sky.

Whispers of day blend with night,
In this dance of dark and light.
The world transforms with each passing hour,
Nature's magic, a fragrant flower.

A Symphony of Hidden Wings

Soft rustles among the leaves,
The songs of wings that the heart believes.
Each flit and flutter tells a tale,
Of freedom's flight on the wind's gale.

In the hush, small creatures play,
In shadows where sunlight sways.
A chorus rises, sweet and clear,
Nature's symphony, always near.

The Guardians of the Glimmering Glade

Ancient trees with wisdom profound,
Stand watch over this sacred ground.
Their roots hold secrets from the past,
In every branch, a story cast.

Starlit nights see their vigil keep,
While the world around them gently sleeps.
These guardians of green, ever true,
In the glade's heart, life anew.

Veils of Green Wrapped in Stillness

In the hush of morning light,
Leaves whisper secrets low,
Softly wrapped in nature's grace,
Veils of green begin to glow.

Silence drapes the forest floor,
As shadows stretch and yawn,
Each blade of grass, a verse untold,
Beneath the waking dawn.

Gentle breezes weave their song,
Through branches high and free,
A tapestry of life unfolds,
In serene harmony.

Stillness holds the world in dreams,
As time begins to pause,
Veils of green, a soft embrace,
Nature's tender cause.

Between the Bark and the Moonlit Sky

Underneath the ancient trees,
Where time stands still and sighs,
The moonlight dances, cool and bright,
Between the bark and skies.

Whispers of the night emerge,
As shadows intertwine,
Each rustle tells a story raw,
In nature's dark design.

Stars are scattered like dreams lost,
In the tapestry of night,
Each flicker holds a mystery,
Boundless in its flight.

The world holds breath, entranced by light,
As wonders softly sprawl,
Between the bark and whispering trees,
Nature's timeless call.

Chronicles of the Woodland Shadows

In the heart of emerald woods,
Where sunlight barely creeps,
Chronicles of shadows weave,
As the forest softly sleeps.

Each branch a tale of ages past,
Of seasons turning slow,
Echoes of the life and love,
In whispers, ebb and flow.

Mossy carpets hold their truths,
While critters roam and play,
In the quiet timeline spun,
Of night eclipsing day.

Here, the past and present blend,
A dance of life anew,
Chronicles of woodland souls,
In shadows' gentle hue.

Dance of the Burgeoning Thorns

Amidst the bloom of vibrant hues,
Thorns cradle beauty rare,
In nature's twist of fate and time,
Life's dance hangs in the air.

Petals soft, yet prickly guards,
Stand sentinel and proud,
Each thorn a lesson, sharp and bright,
Beneath the fragrant shroud.

With every breeze, the flowers sway,
In rhythm with the sun,
A dance of life, a sacred hymn,
As new beginnings run.

Though thorns may pierce, they do not break,
For beauty comes with cost,
In the embrace of thorns and blooms,
Life's balance never lost.

Heartbeats of the Wild

In the forest, whispers sigh,
Leaves rustle as creatures pry.
A gentle call from deep within,
The pulse of life where dreams begin.

Moonlight dances on the stream,
Stars reflect a silent dream.
Footprints trace the path of fate,
In this wild, we all await.

Echoes of a distant roar,
Nature's heart forevermore.
Cicadas hum a lullaby,
Underneath the boundless sky.

With every heartbeat, trees will sway,
Life unfolds in shades of gray.
Here in the wild, we find our peace,
A timeless bond that will not cease.

The Horizon Where Shadows Dance

At dusk, the colors softly blend,
Horizon bends where shadows send.
Whispers linger in the air,
A secret world, both bright and rare.

Silhouettes of trees take flight,
Against the canvas of the night.
Stars awaken, one by one,
As daylight fades, the magic's spun.

Breezes carry stories old,
Of battles fought and dreams retold.
A lingering gaze, a fleeting glance,
Under the spell of shadows' dance.

The horizon shifts, but never breaks,
In this twilight, each heart aches.
For every ending marks a start,
A journey drawn within the heart.

Encounters at Dusk's Edge

As sun dips low, the twilight glows,
Paths converge where silence flows.
Footsteps echo in the night,
Meeting hints of soft moonlight.

Eyes connect, a fleeting spark,
In the stillness, kindred hearts.
Words unspoken fill the air,
In this moment, we're aware.

The world beyond begins to fade,
In shadows, timeless memories laid.
With each breath, a story spun,
Encounters blessed before they're done.

At dusk's edge, the night awaits,
Beneath the stars, two souls create.
In this embrace, we find our place,
A quiet magic, a gentle grace.

Melodies of Moss and Oak

Beneath the boughs of ancient trees,
The air is filled with nature's ease.
Moss carpets ground where footsteps lie,
A symphony of earth and sky.

The rustling leaves compose a tune,
Under the watchful eye of the moon.
Twilight whispers through the glades,
Where every note in silence fades.

Branches sway with rhythmic sway,
In harmony, they gently play.
An orchestra of wood and stone,
In this grove, we're never alone.

Nature's songs, forever new,
In every shade, in every hue.
Moss and oak, a timeless bond,
In these melodies, we respond.

Beneath the Green Veil

In the hush of the morning mist,
Leaves whisper secrets to the dawn.
Sunlight dances on emerald blades,
Nature's ballet on the lawn.

Soft shadows stretch beneath the trees,
Bird songs weave through the gentle air.
A world awakes with quiet ease,
Beneath the green veil, free from care.

The brook sings sweetly, crystal clear,
At its banks, wildflowers bloom bright.
Every step reveals a new sphere,
A tapestry of pure delight.

Come wander here, where dreams take flight,
In this embrace of shade and light.
Let your heart blend with the scene,
Where life unfolds, serene, unseen.

Shadows Among the Pines

Tall silhouettes in silent grace,
Pine trees whisper soft and low.
Amidst their trunks, I find my place,
Where moonlight filters, cool and slow.

A breeze carries tales of the past,
Of days gone by, of night and day.
In shadows dense, memories cast,
They linger, watch, and softly sway.

Beneath their arms, I stand in awe,
Wonders held in every glance.
Nature's beauty without flaw,
Inviting me into its dance.

Here among giants, I feel the peace,
From every worry, a sweet release.
In shadows deep, I find my home,
In the embrace of pines, I roam.

Echoes of an Enchanted Glen

In the heart of the verdant glen,
Magic whispers on the breeze.
Each flower sways, a timeless pen,
Writing tales beyond the trees.

Sunlight spills like golden wine,
Painting colors rare and bold.
Every petal, a sacred sign,
Of stories waiting to be told.

Rippling streams mirror the sky,
Reflecting dreams in silvered light.
As crickets sing their lullaby,
The glen wraps me in gentle night.

Here I linger, lost in thought,
In a world where whispers blend.
Echoes of magic, dearly sought,
In this enchanted glen, my friend.

Mysteries in the Thicket

Twisted branches form a maze,
Secrets murmur in ancient tones.
In the thicket's shadowed gaze,
Life's mysteries weave like unknowns.

Crimson berries catch the eye,
While shadows dance in playful glee.
Each rustle hints at reasons why,
Nature holds her truths so free.

A hidden path beckons me near,
With every step, the air grows dense.
In tangled roots, I'm filled with fear,
Yet drawn to wonder, it feels immense.

Here in the thicket, I find my way,
Through whispers soft and nature's sigh.
Embraced in thorns, I choose to stay,
Mysteries linger, never shy.

The Silence of Leafy Secrets

In the hush of the willow's sway,
Whispers of time drift away.
Shadows dance on the forest floor,
Where nature keeps secrets evermore.

Through tangled vines and ivy's grasp,
Silent stories in silence clasp.
Cautious breezes fill the air,
Carrying tales without a care.

Beneath the rustle of emerald leaves,
Lies the world that nature weaves.
Moonlight peeks through the branches high,
As night unfolds its gentle sigh.

In this haven, peace resides,
Where leafy secrets gently hide.
Listen close, and you may find,
The heart of nature, unconfined.

Trails of Forgotten Dreams

Footsteps linger on winding paths,
Echoing lost longing laughs.
Stars once sparkled in youthful eyes,
Now drift like clouds through dusky skies.

Each corner turned unveils a trace,
Of hopes and fears we once embraced.
Hollow whispers in the gloam,
Call us back to where dreams roam.

Crumbled stones along the route,
Bear witness to a silent shout.
Beneath the weight of passing years,
Forgotten dreams and silent tears.

Yet in the twilight's tender glow,
New dreams await, a gentle flow.
So tread with heart, embrace the night,
For trails can lead to hidden light.

Where the Wildlings Roam

In realms where wildlings dance and play,
Nature hums a wild ballet.
Over hills and under trees,
They weave through life with effortless ease.

With laughter echoing through the glade,
Their footprints mark the forest's shade.
A world untamed, a heart unshackled,
In every rustle, spirit tackled.

They chase the stars where shadows blend,
With fireflies as their only friends.
In dreams, they fly on wings of air,
Crafting magic everywhere.

So join the wildlings, let us roam,
In fields of wonder, we find our home.
Freedom calls in every breeze,
Where hearts align with nature's ease.

Roots of Unseen Stories

Deep below, where shadows dwell,
Roots entwine, a tale to tell.
Secrets buried, change their course,
In silent whispers, nature's force.

Time weaves through the earthy veins,
Carving paths through joys and pains.
Life emerges from unseen ground,
In every thrum, a heartbeat found.

Through twisted roots and tender shoots,
The past sings softly, nature's roots.
From whispered truths to loud applause,
Every story harbors flaws.

So tread lightly where they lie,
Listen close, let spirits fly.
For in the depths of ancient trees,
Lie the roots of histories.

Conversations Among the Dew

Whispers rise with morning light,
Dewdrops dance on petals bright.
Nature's breath, a gentle sigh,
Secrets shared as time slips by.

Each sparkle tells a tale anew,
Of silent nights and skies so blue.
In this realm where stillness reigns,
Language flows through soft refrains.

Through the leaves, their voices glide,
Nature's heart, with purest pride.
In every droplet, stories blend,
Conversations that never end.

Echoes of the Journey Within

Footsteps trace the paths unknown,
In shadows, seeds of wisdom sown.
Each echo carries tales of old,
Whispers from the brave and bold.

In silence dwells a world so vast,
A mirror of the hidden past.
Reflections dance in mind's embrace,
Time and space in fluid grace.

Moments linger, lessons learned,
Fires flicker, passions burned.
Through every twist, the heart remains,
Echoes of the journey's gains.

Embraced by Twisted Pathways

Winding trails through ancient woods,
Where time flows like tender floods.
Every turn, a new surprise,
In tangled roots, the spirit lies.

Branches reach with open arms,
Embracing nature's peaceful charms.
Lost and found in pathways wild,
An adventure waits, like a curious child.

Guided by the stars above,
Through every twist, I find my love.
In the embrace of mystery's art,
Each step unfolds a brand new start.

The Stories Written in Light and Shadow

Beneath the sun, the stories gleam,
While shadows weave a whispered dream.
In every glow, a hope is spun,
As day and night become as one.

Words like sunlight dance and play,
Casting warmth through every day.
In twilight's hush, the tales arise,
Secrets hidden beneath the skies.

Gathered in the dusk's embrace,
Life's sketches find their place.
In light and shadow's gentle flow,
The stories live, the stories grow.

Whispers Beneath the Canopy

Leaves murmur softly above,
In the hush where secrets dwell,
Nature's breath, a gentle shove,
Breathing stories it won't tell.

Sunlight dances through the green,
Casting dreams on woodland floors,
Each shadow holds a world unseen,
Where the heart finds open doors.

Rustling whispers weave like lace,
In this serene, enchanting space,
Echoes linger, hearts embrace,
Underneath the sky's warm grace.

Moments trapped in time's embrace,
In the woodland's quiet song,
Every heartbeat holds a trace,
Of a place where we belong.

Shadows of the Emerald Grove

Beneath the boughs, the shadows play,
Flickering in the dusk's soft light,
Each step reveals the hidden way,
In emerald hues, both dark and bright.

The ground is thick with whispered tales,
Of creatures seen and those unseen,
Through winding paths where silence trails,
And every glance unveils a dream.

Mossy stones and twisted roots,
Guard the secrets of the night,
Nature's cloak, in vibrant suits,
Wraps the world in soft delight.

In this grove, where shadows dance,
Time stands still, a gentle sway,
Each moment blooms, given the chance,
To linger longer, come what may.

Secrets of the Wooded Veil

Through the mist where silence lies,
Whispers curl like curling smoke,
Each breath a tale, a soft disguise,
The trees are sages, never spoke.

Veiled in green, a mystic shroud,
Secrets woven in the air,
Among their trunks, quiet and proud,
Wisdom blooms with utmost care.

Shade and light in harmony,
Choreograph the forest's breath,
In this realm of mystery,
Life and death, an endless depth.

Every path holds echoes faint,
Of journeys lost and stories found,
In the woodland's timeless paint,
Imprinted deep within the ground.

Echoes Among the Ancient Trees

Beneath the boughs where time stands still,
Ancient giants rise with grace,
Whispers linger, trails to fill,
In their arms, we find our place.

Roots entwined, a sacred bond,
Each ring a story, deep and wide,
Of seasons changed and those beyond,
Of life and death in nature's tide.

Echoes carry through the air,
Songs of old, they softly call,
In the solace, we lay bare,
The truth reflected in it all.

From towering crowns to earthly floor,
In this haven, we explore,
Among the aged, we restore,
The memories we cherish more.

Beyond the Gnarled Branches

Whispers dance in twilight's glow,
Where secrets hide, and shadows grow.
Beneath the stars' attentive gaze,
The night reveals its tangled maze.

A breeze weaves tales from days of old,
In every sigh, a story's told.
Gnarled branches, like fingers, reach,
To grasp the dreams that spirits preach.

Silvery mist envelops the path,
Guiding hearts through nature's wrath.
In intimate silence, souls convene,
Where all that's lost may still be seen.

So linger here, let time stand still,
Beyond the branches, feel the thrill.
In the embrace of the night so fair,
Find your truth in the chilling air.

Moonlight on Mossy Ground

Soft moonlight blankets the glade,
A gentle touch where shadows fade.
Mossy carpets, lush and bright,
Whisper secrets to the night.

Each silver beam, a lover's call,
Inviting dreams to rise and fall.
Nature's heart beats steady and slow,
In the silence, pure feelings flow.

Crickets sing their serenade,
As night unfolds a grand parade.
Stars wink bright in velvet skies,
While owls watch with knowing eyes.

Here among the ancient trees,
Feel the pulse of the evening breeze.
In the magic of this hour,
Embrace the night, let spirit flower.

Serpentines of the Ancient Wood

Through serpentines the path does wind,
To realms where whispers intertwine.
The ancient wood holds tales untold,
In every leaf, a memory bold.

Branches sway in gentle grace,
As shadows dance, the spirits embrace.
Soft rustles hint at what may come,
In the heartbeat of the forest's hum.

Beneath the boughs, the world is still,
Chasing dreams with quiet thrill.
Twisted roots and fragrant air,
Hold the stories that linger there.

So wander deep, let the wood unfold,
Embrace the beauty of the old.
In every bend, a lesson learned,
In ancient paths, the heart is turned.

Veiled Pathways of the Earth

Veiled pathways lie beneath the mist,
Each step a sigh, each twist a tryst.
In shadows deep, the secrets wait,
For curious souls to contemplate.

Softly tread on nature's skin,
Where stories of the earth begin.
With every bend, a hidden view,
A world reborn in shades of hue.

Muffled sounds of whispers low,
Echo tales of those who know.
In this haven of whispered lore,
Feel the magic at your core.

So journey forth on paths unseen,
Embrace the quiet, feel the green.
In the veils of earth, find your way,
Where every dawn is a new day.

Sylvan Secrets Unraveled

In the woods where shadows play,
Whispers of the night convey,
A tale of leaves and hidden streams,
Where nature breathes and softly dreams.

Mossy paths where secrets lie,
Carried by the breeze nearby,
Trees embrace with ancient lore,
Calling souls to seek and explore.

Sunlight dapples on the ground,
Painting stories all around,
In every rustle, sigh, and sound,
The heartbeat of the wild is found.

A journey deep where wonders spark,
Each step a note, a vibrant mark,
Sylvan realms await the brave,
In enchanted whispers, nature's grave.

Beneath the Leaves of Mystery

Underneath the emerald boughs,
Where secrets form and nature bows,
Shadows dance in twilight's glow,
Beneath the leaves, the stories flow.

Whispers carried on the air,
Hints of magic lingering there,
With every rustle, tales unfold,
Of ancient paths and dreams untold.

Crimson berries, hidden tight,
Guiding wanderers in the night,
Each step a note in nature's song,
In the wild, where hearts belong.

A tapestry of green unfolds,
As dusk embraces, courage molds,
Beneath the leaves, the world awakes,
In the silence, magic stakes.

Enchanted Byways of Green

On paths where sunlight gently weaves,
A dance of shadows, a tale it leaves,
Through meadows lush, where wildflowers bloom,
The heart finds solace, the spirit's room.

In twilight's hush, the fireflies gleam,
Life's mysteries wrap like a dream,
Every turn a glance at fate,
In nature's arms, our hopes await.

Winding trails through ancient trees,
Each whisper held by the teasing breeze,
In the thicket, where echoes twine,
Past and present beautifully align.

Enchanted byways beckon near,
With every step, we shed our fear,
In the green embrace of wild terrain,
The heart finds peace, like gentle rain.

The Lure of the Leafy Abyss

In shadows deep, the silence hums,
Through tangled roots, adventure comes,
Veils of green that softly cling,
A world unveiled, where nature sings.

Buried secrets yearn to rise,
In leafy depths, beneath the skies,
Echoes of laughter, memories swirl,
In the abyss, the dreams unfurl.

A tapestry woven with light and shade,
In every whisper, the past is laid,
With every heartbeat, stories breathe,
In the lure of leaves, our hearts believe.

The dance of shadows, the call of the wild,
In nature's arms, we become a child,
Embraced by the forest, forever we roam,
In the leafy abyss, we find our home.

Mysteries Lurking Beneath the Underbrush

In shadows deep, the silence breathes,
Where secrets hide among the leaves.
Roots intertwine, a web of fate,
Alluring paths we can't await.

Fungi bloom in colors bright,
An unseen world out of sight.
Critters dance in twilight's glow,
Each twist and turn, we long to know.

Beneath the soil, soft whispers spin,
Tales of life where none have been.
With every step, the forest calls,
Mysteries left behind the walls.

Beneath the brush, the stories weave,
A hidden realm that we believe.
In every sound, a riddle lies,
Awaiting hearts, where wonder flies.

Journey to the Heart of the Leafy Enigma

Beneath the green, the journey starts,
With hidden truths that share our hearts.
Enchanted paths invite our tread,
In leaves of gold, the old ones said.

Branches arch like ancient lore,
Leading us to a secret shore.
A rustling sound, a fleeting flight,
In this embrace, we chase the light.

With every breath, the canopy sighs,
Revealing worlds beneath the skies.
Shaded groves, where spirits dance,
In nature's arms, we melt in trance.

The leafy whispers pull us near,
An enigma wrapped in ancient cheer.
Through tangled limbs, our questions rise,
In quest for truth, our spirits fly.

Whispers of the Canopy

High above, the branches sway,
The canopy holds secrets at bay.
Leaves shimmer with a gentle grace,
Inviting dreams to weave their lace.

Breezes carry softest songs,
Of feathered friends who belong.
In shadows cast, the stories spark,
Echos found, a dance in the dark.

From heights we see a world anew,
Each whisper shared, a bond so true.
In gentle rustles, magic spins,
A sacred space where life begins.

Beneath the stars, the night unfolds,
Mysteries in the air, untold.
In every breath, a world to seek,
The whispers call, the heart will speak.

Secrets Beneath the Bark

Beneath rough skin, the stories dwell,
In time's embrace, they weave their spell.
Layers of life, worn and wise,
Holding echoes, ancient ties.

The sap flows forth with tales of yore,
Quiet strength at nature's core.
Among the rings, the years unspool,
Lessons learned, where silence rules.

In cracks and crevices, life will bloom,
A fragile dance defying gloom.
Mossy carpets, soft and deep,
Whispered secrets, the forest keeps.

With every knock, a story wakes,
In bark's embrace, the heart it quakes.
Layers thick with life and fate,
In every tree, a world awaits.

The Puzzle of Twilight's Edge

Fragments of day start to fade,
Whispers of night softly invade.
Shadows stretch in gentle dance,
A fleeting glimpse, a lost chance.

Crescent moon in velvet sky,
Painting dreams as stars drift by.
A riddle wrapped in dusk's embrace,
Where secrets hide and time finds space.

Colors merge in soft twilight,
A canvas brushed with fading light.
Each breath a note in evening's song,
In this puzzle, we all belong.

Mysteries in the air unfold,
Stories waiting to be told.
At twilight's edge, we pause and stare,
Unlock the night with whispered prayer.

Chambers of Leafy Reverie

In the woodland's hush, time slows,
Where sunlight dapples, and soft wind blows.
Leaves embrace in a gentle sway,
A secret world where dreams can play.

Echoes of laughter among the trees,
Nature's hush sings melodies.
Shadows dance on the forest floor,
An endless tale forevermore.

Branches sway in sweet delight,
Guided by the stars so bright.
Every rustle, a story spun,
In chambers where the wild things run.

Moments linger, the heart takes flight,
Embracing all in nature's light.
In leafy nooks where echoes thrive,
We find the magic, feel alive.

Roots Digging into Time

Beneath the soil, secrets lie,
Whispers of ages, silent sighs.
Roots entwined, they tell the tale,
Of growth and strife, of light and veil.

Years unfold in patterns vast,
Echoes of futures, shadows of past.
Nature's grip, both firm and kind,
In every twist, a truth to find.

Branches stretch toward the skies,
While roots delve deep with ancient sighs.
Timeless wonders, quiet and bold,
In every heartbeat, stories told.

Through storms and sun, they intertwine,
A tapestry of life divine.
With every season, wisdom grows,
In the dance of time, the heart knows.

Lanterns of the Silent Night

Flickers glow in the velvet dark,
Guiding dreams like a gentle spark.
Whispers linger on the cool breeze,
Carrying tales through swaying trees.

Stars like lanterns fill the sky,
Painting wishes that drift and fly.
Night wraps all in a soft embrace,
Every moment holds a grace.

Shadows play on the dim-lit ground,
Crickets sing their serenade sound.
In the silence, hearts take flight,
Finding solace in the night.

Underneath the moon's soft gaze,
Lost in wonder, in night's maze.
Each lantern a hope, a gentle light,
Illuminating dreams in quiet night.

Where Light Dances with Shade

In the forest where shadows play,
Sunbeams flicker, bright and gay.
Leaves whisper secrets, soft and low,
As the gentle breezes blow.

Moss carpets the ground, lush and deep,
While the world around begins to sleep.
Colors blend in a tender embrace,
Nature's artistry in every place.

Birds serenade from branches high,
Echoing dreams, as time flits by.
Moments linger in golden streams,
Where reality intertwines with dreams.

Here in this realm where shadows glide,
Life's tender pulse cannot hide.
As light and shade in harmony meet,
Creation dances at nature's feet.

Odes to the Overgrown Realm

In a tangle of vines and verdant green,
Whispers of life can often be seen.
Each petal holds tales of days gone past,
In this wild world, nothing is fast.

A symphony played by the rustling leaves,
Nature's music, quiet heart that grieves.
Here, the thorns and blooms intertwine,
A woven tapestry, both fierce and divine.

In every corner, a story unfolds,
The ancient secrets the forest holds.
From hidden nooks to sun-drenched glades,
Life flourishes boldly, never fades.

Ode to the overgrown, untamed and free,
In this wildness lies tranquility.
Through tangled roots, the heart finds peace,
A sacred promise that will never cease.

Twilight's Embrace in the Thicket

As the sun dips low and shadows bloom,
Twilight whispers through the gloom.
In the thicket where secrets stay,
Evening melts the light away.

Crickets serenade the gathering night,
Stars awaken, twinkling bright.
A soft hush drapes the world anew,
In twilight's arms, dreams drift through.

The air thickens with a sweet perfume,
Nature's palette in deepening gloom.
Every rustle, a story to tell,
In the thicket where magic dwells.

Wrapped in quiet, the heart beats slow,
In twilight's embrace, let worries go.
For here in the dusk, all things align,
An enchantment, gentle and divine.

Beneath the Boughs of Silence

Underneath the ancient trees,
Time stands still with whispered ease.
Branches arch like arms of grace,
In this sacred, peaceful space.

Silence blankets the forest floor,
Echoing tales of ages sore.
Every rustling leaf and sigh,
Holds the wisdom of the sky.

Mushrooms peep from under the shade,
Nature's beauty never fades.
In stillness, the heart finds its place,
Beneath the boughs, a warm embrace.

Listen closely; the echoes call,
In this haven, we find it all.
Under the trees, in nature's fold,
Stories of silence quietly told.

Fragments of Sunlight and Shadow

In the forest where whispers blend,
Fragments of sunlight start to bend.
Shadows stretch and dance around,
In this magic, peace is found.

Leaves rustle softly in the breeze,
Creating echoes of ancient trees.
Where light kisses the forest floor,
Nature sings forevermore.

Glimmers of gold through branches peek,
Where secrets hide and silence speaks.
Embracing warmth, the coolness flows,
In gentle waves, the spirit grows.

Moments captured, fading fast,
In twilight dreams, our souls are cast.
A tapestry of light and dark,
In every corner, nature's spark.

Sipping from Nature's Cup

With every sip of morning dew,
The world awakens, fresh and new.
In crystal drops, the sun's delight,
Nature's gifts, so pure and bright.

Leaves glisten with the dawn's embrace,
Each moment holds a sacred space.
A floral brew that hums and sings,
In harmony, all living things.

The wind carries a sweet perfume,
In nature's heart, we find our room.
From petals soft to rivers wide,
In every sip, we feel the tide.

Gathering whispers, we align,
With earth's embrace, our spirits shine.
Sipping from this cup divine,
In nature's lap, we intertwine.

Flower Petals in the Dark

In midnight's calm, petals unfold,
Whispers of beauty, stories told.
Fragile dreams in shadows sway,
Delicate blooms that softly play.

Moonlight casts a silver hue,
On silent gardens, dipped in dew.
Night's embrace holds secrets tight,
Floral secrets in the night.

Fleeting scents in twilight air,
Softly drifting, free from care.
In such stillness, hearts can hark,
To the gentle, glowing spark.

Life awakens while we sleep,
In the darkness, promises keep.
Flower petals, a sleeping charm,
Guarding dreams with tender calm.

Veils of Green Mystery

In the woods where secrets lie,
Veils of green brush by, oh my!
Nature cloaked in hues so deep,
Whispers linger, hush to keep.

Mossy carpets, soft underfoot,
In every step, a hidden root.
The world sways in shadow and light,
Enigmas dance, both bold and slight.

Beneath the ferns, a life untold,
In tangled growth, the stories unfold.
A symphony of rustling leaves,
In veils of green, the heart believes.

Through emerald halls, we wander free,
In nature's cradle, spirits flee.
With every breath, we feel the call,
In mystery's arms, we find our all.

Songs of the Lost Canopy

Whispers weave through ancient trees,
Echoes of a time long past.
Leaves rustle with hidden tales,
Their secrets held firm and fast.

In shadows deep, their voices blend,
Melodies of twilight's song.
A symphony of life unseen,
In the canopy, where we belong.

Feathered friends on branches sway,
Nightingales in soft refrain.
They sing of journeys, lost and found,
In melodies of joy and pain.

But as the light begins to fade,
The songs grow faint, the colors dim.
Yet in the heart, their sounds remain,
A lullaby, a cherished hymn.

Spirits of the Woodland Depths

In the hush of emerald halls,
Spirits dance with gentle grace.
Mossy floors and tangled vines,
Guard their time and sacred space.

Beneath the boughs, the shadows play,
Glowing eyes in dusky light.
They guide the lost and weary hearts,
Through the depths of silent night.

The air is thick with ancient lore,
Carried softly on the breeze.
Whispers woven in twilight's thread,
Granting solace, bringing peace.

In every rustle, a tale unfolds,
Of lives entwined and dreams set free.
The woodland spirits, patient guides,
Hold the keys to mystery.

Retreat of the Twilight Creatures

As daylight dims and shadows grow,
Creatures stir from hidden places.
With every rustle, soft and low,
The twilight cloak their gentle graces.

Owls take flight on silent wings,
Moonlit paths their secret claim.
Foxes dart through dusky rings,
In the dance of night, they play their game.

In the hush, the crickets sing,
A lullaby of dusk's embrace.
Bats flit by on shadowed wing,
In rhythm with the night's swift pace.

Emerge they do, in soft retreat,
From sunlit days to evening's call.
In twilight's grace, their hearts will meet,
The night belongs to one and all.

An Invisible Sanctuary

In the heart of the forest wild,
Lies a space where spirits dwell.
Hidden paths, a dreamlike child,
Where worries fade and peace will swell.

Glimmers of light break through the green,
Each beam a welcome, soft and warm.
A sanctuary, rarely seen,
Cradles all in nature's charm.

Birdsong echoes through the air,
Wrapped in whispers of the leaves.
Moments linger, free from care,
In this place, the heart believes.

Though unseen by hurried eyes,
It shelters those who seek to find.
In the stillness, soul replies,
A haven for the quiet mind.

A Tapestry of Diverging Paths

In shadows where the choices lie,
Footsteps whisper, time drifts by.
Threads of fate in twilight spun,
A tapestry with colors run.

Each road unveils a hidden door,
Unraveled tales on distant shore.
Winds of change beckon, sweet and deep,
As dreams awaken from their sleep.

With every turn, a story blooms,
In vibrant hues, the heart consumes.
A path once taken, never lost,
Our choices marked, whatever the cost.

So let us walk with open eyes,
Embrace the dawn, the fading skies.
For in the weave of chance we find,
The beauty of the curious mind.

Dreams Woven in Ferns

In woodland whispers, secrets stir,
A dance of dreams in ferns that blur.
Softly swaying, they catch the light,
Infinite tales in the hush of night.

Each leaf a canvas, stories told,
Of hearts entwined and spirits bold.
Among the undergrowth we find,
A haven for the wandering mind.

The murmur of a hidden stream,
Flows softly through the dreamer's dream.
As moonbeams lace with shadows cast,
We weave our futures from the past.

In this lush haven, let us hear,
The sonnets spun, the joys sincere.
Dreams woven in ferns, tightly bound,
In nature's cradle, true magic found.

Nestled Among Ancient Sentinels

Beneath the boughs of giants old,
Whispers of time in silence told.
Nestled among the sentinels' gaze,
Life unfolds in a magical haze.

Mossy carpets where shadows meet,
In every corner, stories greet.
Echoes of wisdom in the air,
A sanctuary, free from care.

The roots entwined, a web so wide,
Hold secrets of the earth and tide.
Among these giants, dreams take flight,
In tranquil realms, bathed in light.

Each breeze a sigh, each rustle a tune,
Guided by stars, beneath the moon.
Here, in stillness, hearts align,
Nestled among the ancient pine.

The Ciphers of Twisting Vines

In gardens where the willows weep,
Twisting vines in silence creep.
Winding stories on the ground,
In nature's arms, the truth is found.

Each curl and knot, a silent clue,
Of journeys traveled, old and new.
A cipher spun in emerald hue,
Unlocks the whispers known to few.

The tendrils dance, alive and free,
A symphony of earth's decree.
Beneath the sun, beneath the shade,
Tales of love and loss portrayed.

In tangled webs, we write our fate,
With every twist, we celebrate.
The ciphers known to hearts that seek,
A legacy of souls unique.

Dwellers of the Silent Glade

In a glade where whispers dwell,
Shadows dance, casting spells.
Leaves that murmur, secrets shared,
Life in silence, unaware.

Moonlight drapes the peaceful night,
Stars above, a distant sight.
Crickets sing their lullabies,
Nature's calm, no need for lies.

Fern and moss, a carpet green,
Echoes of what's seldom seen.
Creatures roam with gentle grace,
Time slows down in this safe space.

When dawn breaks, the magic fades,
Yet the heart knows where it wades.
Return, we shall, to love's embrace,
In the glade, our sacred place.

Elusive Beasts in the Underbrush

In the thicket, shadows flit,
Mysteries in twilit grit.
Eyes that glimmer, quick and sly,
In the dusk, they dance and fly.

Paws that pad on silent ground,
In the darkness, they are found.
Silent watchers, robed in night,
Making moments pure delight.

Whispers of the forest speak,
Tales of creatures, shy and meek.
Hidden paths and soft retreat,
Nature's joy, a soft heartbeat.

In the hush, we catch a glance,
Of these beasts who roam and prance.
Elusive wonders of the wood,
In the shadows, all is good.

The Language of Rustling Foliage

Leaves converse in subtle tones,
Songs of branches, ancient bones.
Wind carries their whispered sighs,
A dialogue beneath the skies.

Every rustle tells a tale,
Of hidden lives that never pale.
Secrets wrapped in emerald hues,
Nature's language, soft and true.

Breeze that brings a gentle shake,
Conversations for nature's sake.
Listen close, the stories flow,
In the woods, the secrets grow.

Through the oaks, their voices weave,
Telling all who dare believe.
Language of the wild, so bright,
Rustling foliage, day and night.

Chasing Sunbeams Through the Trees

Sunlight filters, golden rays,
Dancing in the leafy maze.
Chasing shadows, bright and bold,
Warmth of day begins to unfold.

Through the canopy, we run,
Laughter echoes, hearts like spun.
Every beam a tale to tell,
Where the forest dreams so well.

Footsteps light on soft, cool ground,
Nature's whispers all around.
As we chase the fading light,
In the trees, our spirits bright.

When the twilight starts to creep,
In our hearts, the joy we keep.
Chasing sunbeams, wild and free,
In the woods, it's you and me.

Secrets Woven in Roots and Vines

In shadows deep where whispers twine,
Silent tales of old entwine.
Beneath the earth, the stories creep,
Through tangled roots, they softly seep.

Veins of green in twilight's hold,
Guard the secrets never told.
Each tendril holds a whispered prayer,
A mystery woven in the air.

In shrouded nooks, enchantments brew,
With every branch, the secrets grew.
Underneath the starry skies,
Nature's voice softly replies.

So pause awhile where shadows dance,
Embrace the magic, take a chance.
For in the silence, truth will find,
The whispers of the root and vine.

The Lush Labyrinth Beneath

In a realm where shadows weave,
The lush labyrinth starts to breathe.
Each pathway formed by gentle grace,
Hides a world in a secret space.

Roots entwined like stories shared,
Every turn, a vision bared.
Mossy carpets span the ground,
In the stillness, magic's found.

Creeping vines and fragrant loam,
Echo softest calls of home.
Nature's maze, both wild and free,
Holds the heart of mystery.

So wander through this verdant art,
Let its wonder fill your heart.
The lush labyrinth leads the way,
To realms where night dissolves to day.

Murmurs of the Mysterious Canopy

Above the world, where spirits play,
The canopy whispers night and day.
Leaves flutter tales of ages past,
In the green, shadows are cast.

Branches sway with gentle grace,
Guardians of this sacred place.
In sunlight's glow, secrets bloom,
Murmurs echo in the gloom.

With every rustle, stories rise,
The voice of nature never lies.
Underneath the emerald dome,
The heart beats wild, the trees call home.

So listen close to the soft refrain,
In the emerald maze, joy and pain.
For in this dance of leaf and light,
The ancient whispers take their flight.

Soliloquies of the Enchanted Glade

In the heart of the woodland's grace,
The glade sings in a soft embrace.
With every breeze, a tale unfolds,
In whispers shared that never grow old.

Sunbeams waltz on emerald blades,
Illuminating nature's aids.
Petals sigh as they drop down,
Each moment drapes a treasure crown.

Here creatures pause, the world stands still,
In the glade, time bends to will.
Where wildflowers dance and sway,
Echoes of beauty gently play.

So linger where the silence hums,
Listen closely as nature drums.
In the enchanted space, spirits glide,
A serenade where dreams abide.

Echoing Footsteps in Green Halls

In the forest deep, shadows play,
Leaves dance softly, leading the way.
Footsteps echo, a whispered song,
Nature's chorus where I belong.

Sunlight filters through whispers bright,
Painting the ground in dappled light.
Every step a story, every breath
Embraces life, defying death.

Through winding paths, the spirits glide,
In this sanctuary, fears subside.
Mossy stones and ancient trees,
Hold the secrets carried by the breeze.

In the heart of green, moments blend,
Time stands still, a faithful friend.
With every whisper, the world unfolds,
In nature's arms, pure magic holds.

The Riddle of Whispering Pines

Whispers rise from needle-lined bows,
Secrets spoken where the soft wind flows.
Pines hold tales of ages past,
In their embrace, shadows are cast.

Underneath this emerald dome,
The trees invite you, seek your home.
Through rustling leaves, questions arise,
Seeking answers beneath the skies.

Footsteps lead to hidden trails,
Where mystery weaves and curiosity prevails.
Each crackling branch, a voice so clear,
Reveals the riddles, drawing near.

In twilight's hush, the answers gleam,
Life's deeper truths drift like a dream.
Nature's puzzle, a map so fine,
The heart listens, and all aligns.

Hidden Reflections of the Sky

Beneath the surface, worlds appear,
Mirrored skies hold wisdom dear.
Rippled waters share their grace,
Capturing dreams in fluid space.

Clouds drift softly, stories told,
Each reflection a glimpse of gold.
In ponds and streams, the heavens blend,
Preparing for the day to end.

In quiet moments, the sky reveals,
Truths that linger, and time heals.
A canvas painted with light and shade,
Where thoughts unfold, and fears they fade.

As twilight draws the curtain low,
Hidden reflections begin to glow.
With every glance, the heart can see,
The boundless wonders of what may be.

Nooks Where Time Stands Still

In secret corners, forgotten nooks,
The air is thick with untold books.
Pages whisper tales of old,
In quiet moments, treasures unfold.

Sunbeams filter through dusty glass,
Memory dances, moments pass.
Each crack in the wall tells a tale,
Of laughter, whispers, love's sweet trail.

Here, time halts, the world fades away,
In these havens, dreams start to sway.
Echoes of laughter linger near,
Steeped in silence, solace clear.

Find your heart in these sacred places,
In stillness, life's true beauty graces.
In the nooks where time stands still,
Beauty awakens, and hearts are filled.

Enigma of the Woodland Whisper

Through tangled trees the secrets sigh,
In shadows where the soft winds lie.
A melody of ancient tales,
Whispers call from hidden trails.

Beneath the boughs where silence weaves,
A dance of light among the leaves.
Curiosity lingers near,
An echo of what we hold dear.

Moonlit paths and twilight gleams,
Awake the heart with forgotten dreams.
In every rustle, every glance,
The woodland holds its mystic dance.

So heed the whispers, light and free,
In enigma's arms, we long to be.
In nature's grasp, the truth will show,
Where every secret yearns to flow.

The Tapestry of Nature's Embrace

In vibrant hues the world unfolds,
A canvas where the story holds.
Each flower's breath a whispered song,
In nature's weave we all belong.

The mountains stand with watchful pride,
Their majesty cannot subside.
Through valleys deep and rivers wide,
Life's masterpiece does here abide.

With every dawn, new colors blend,
As day and night gracefully mend.
From sunlit groves to starry skies,
Nature's art forever flies.

We wander through this silent space,
Enchanted by the warm embrace.
In every thread of life we trace,
A tapestry of love's sweet grace.

Guardian Spirits of the Sun-dappled Grove

In sunlight's glow, the spirits dance,
Among the trees, a sacred chance.
With every rustle, heartbeats clear,
They guide our paths, they hold us near.

Their gentle whispers touch the air,
In ancient woods, we find them there.
With eyes of wisdom, voices pure,
They cherish life, they make us sure.

At twilight's edge, they softly sing,
Of nature's gifts and all they bring.
In every shadow, every light,
Their guardianship enhances sight.

Feel their warmth, the gentle plea,
To cherish nature endlessly.
In sun-dappled groves, our spirits rise,
Bound together, 'neath endless skies.

Phantoms in the Thicket

In tangled roots where shadows creep,
The phantoms gather, secrets keep.
Their fleeting forms a wisp of mist,
In thickets dense, they coexist.

With glowing eyes, they watch and wait,
A silent bond, a twisted fate.
In moonlit dawns, they shimmer near,
Chasing dreams with subtle fear.

They carry tales of days long past,
Of love and loss, of shadows cast.
Each rustling leaf, a ghostly sigh,
Echoes of the years gone by.

In thickets dark, the spirits roam,
With every song, they find a home.
Embrace the whispers of the night,
For phantoms bring their mystic light.

Dappled Shadows and Luminous Glimmers

Beneath the boughs, shadows play,
Sunlight dances, bright and gay.
Leaves flutter softly in the breeze,
Whispers of nature, moments seize.

Luminous glimmers on the stream,
Reflecting the sky's gentle dream.
Ripples carry tales from afar,
Carving secrets where dreams are star.

Patterns shift in nature's light,
Crafting wonders, day and night.
In this realm, magic spills,
Enchanting hearts, the spirit thrills.

Dappled shadows softly sway,
Guiding us along the way.
Every glance reveals the gift,
In stillness, thoughts begin to lift.

The Enigma of Twilight Glades

In twilight glades, a hush prevails,
Mysteries hid in shadowed trails.
Silhouettes blend, their edges blurred,
As nature softly speaks, unheard.

Moonlight spills on the forest floor,
Lighting paths we can't ignore.
Every shadow holds a tale,
Of timeless truths that softly sail.

Between the dusk and dawn's first glow,
Whispers weave through branches low.
In the stillness, secrets sigh,
Enigmas linger, never die.

Hearts entwined with nature's grace,
In twilight's arms, we find our place.
Each breath a dance, so calm, so free,
In the glades, forever we'll be.

Spirits of the Whispering Leaves

Amidst the trees, they softly call,
Spirits dance, so free, enthrall.
Whispering secrets, tales untold,
In every rustle, life unfolds.

Leaves shimmer in the gentle light,
Echoing laughter, a pure delight.
Nature's symphony, sweet and clear,
Voices of the lost draw near.

Cascades of green, a sacred space,
Where time stands still, and dreams embrace.
Listen closely, lend your ear,
To the songs that nature holds dear.

In the grove where shadows play,
Spirit leaves dance and sway.
Every sigh, a story weaves,
Beckoning souls, the whispering leaves.

Fragments of Nature's Embrace

In fractured light, the world refrains,
Nature's beauty, soft as strains.
Fragments glisten, a canvas bright,
Each moment captured, pure delight.

Petals flutter in the breeze,
Carried gently, like whispered pleas.
Echoes linger in warmest air,
Nature's art is everywhere.

Through every crack, the wild blooms,
In vibrant hues, dispelling glooms.
From broken paths to verdant ways,
Life finds strength in all that stays.

Embrace the fragments, let them guide,
In nature's heart, we will abide.
In every piece, a story finds,
The bond of earth with searching minds.

Nature's Cloaked Sanctuary

In whispers soft, the leaves do sway,
A haven where the wild things play.
Beneath the boughs, in shadows cast,
The secrets of the forest last.

The sunlight filters through the green,
A tranquil sight, a peaceful scene.
Each rustle tells a tale untold,
Of life and love in nature's fold.

The fragrant blooms in colors bright,
Invite the weary to take flight.
In every corner, beauty lies,
A sanctuary 'neath the skies.

Here time stands still, as moments blend,
In nature's arms, the soul can mend.
A cloaked embrace, a gentle nudge,
In sanctuary, we find our judge.

Sibilant Songs of the Undergrowth

The gentle rustle of the leaves,
A symphony the forest weaves.
In shadows deep, where whispers roam,
The undergrowth feels like a home.

Crickets chirp and soft winds sigh,
Their melodies fill up the sky.
A chorus sung by hidden things,
As nature's voice of solace rings.

The ferns unfurl their secret tales,
In vibrant green, where magic prevails.
Each sound a note in nature's score,
A sibilant call forevermore.

Together they create a song,
In perfect harmony, they belong.
Listen close, and you might find,
The music of the heart, entwined.

Heartbeats of the Forgotten Woods

In ancient trees, the heartbeats thrum,
A pulse of life, a distant drum.
Forgotten paths of time away,
Where echoes of the past still play.

Amidst the roots, a story's spun,
Of battles lost and victories won.
The air is thick with memories,
A tapestry of mysteries.

With every step, a ghostly dance,
Of spirits caught in fate's own chance.
Heartbeats linger on the breeze,
Whispering through the ancient trees.

In silent woods, the past awakes,
As time within the stillness breaks.
Every heartbeat tells a tale,
In nature's realm where spirits sail.

Veiled Pathways in Verdant Halls

The path ahead, a winding maze,
In verdant halls, where sunlight plays.
Beneath the arch of emerald trees,
The secrets drift upon the breeze.

With every twist, the wild unfolds,
A story whispered, softly told.
The ferns embrace, the shadows dance,
Inviting all to take a chance.

The scent of moss and earth unite,
In harmony, both day and night.
Veiled pathways sing of days long past,
In nature's arms, forever cast.

As footsteps tread on ancient ground,
The gentle silence wraps around.
In these halls where green prevails,
The heart finds peace, as joy inhales.

Beneath the Soft Canopy

Whispers of leaves in the gentle breeze,
Soft shadows dance with such quiet ease.
Sunlight filters through branches above,
Nature cradles all with tender love.

Moss carpets the ground, a lush, green bed,
While birds in the treetops sing overhead.
The world feels calm, wrapped in a soft sigh,
Beneath the vast blue, where dreams drift and fly.

In this serene spot, worries drift away,
Time slows its pace, in the light of day.
Each heartbeat echoes with nature's song,
In this peaceful place, where we all belong.

With every step, the forest calls near,
In moments like these, nothing seems clear.
Caught in a web of green foliage light,
We lose ourselves in the soft, pure delight.

Hidden Lives of the Woodland

Among the trees, shadows weave their tale,
Silent creatures roam in the dappled vale.
Echoes of paws leave no trace behind,
In the woodland's heart, secrets unwind.

Burrows and nests cradle lives unknown,
The rustle of leaves tells stories alone.
A flick of a tail, a soft whispered sound,
Hidden lives flourish, together unbound.

In twilight's glow, the magic ignites,
With owls that call on the cool, dark nights.
Hush softly, listen; the world's alive,
In these hidden realms, the wild things thrive.

A dance of the ferns sways with the breeze,
Nature's embrace in the boughs of the trees.
With every heartbeat, a pulse so divine,
In the woodland's arms, the secret's entwined.

Journeying Through the Green Labyrinth

Winding paths beckon, secrets to unveil,
Through emerald arches, we set our sail.
Twisting and turning, lost in the maze,
Where sunlight filters through forest ablaze.

Each rustling leaf tells stories of old,
Mysteries whispered, adventures unfold.
Footsteps on trails carved by time's gentle hand,
Journeying onward through this lush land.

With every turn, new wonders await,
Spirits of nature open the gate.
Lost in this maze, we dance with the light,
In the heart of the wood, our souls take flight.

Emerging at dusk, the world wrapped in gold,
Every moment cherished, each one a bold hold.
In the labyrinth green, where life intertwines,
We find our way home, through the ancient pines.

Secrets of the Silent Grove

In the heart of the grove, stillness resides,
Mystery whispers where shadow abides.
Ancient trees stand, guardians in time,
Keeping their secrets, a rhythm, a rhyme.

Sunlit glimmers dance on the forest floor,
Footfalls unheard, as we seek to explore.
Echoes of stories in the echoing bark,
In the silent grove, we wander, embark.

With each gentle rustle, the silence awakes,
Nature's soft breath, the hush gently breaks.
Beneath the thick canopy, calmness does reign,
In the grove's quietude, we feel no pain.

A sanctuary waiting, a space to reflect,
Where the heart finds solace, and thoughts can connect.
Amongst the tall sentinels, wisdom flows free,
In the secrets concealed, we discover what's me.

Breaths of the Forgotten

In whispers soft, the echoes sleep,
Of tales untold, in silence deep.
A memory lingers, lost in time,
Nestled in shadows, a fleeting rhyme.

Through dusty paths, the phantoms stride,
Where dreams entwine, and hopes abide.
Fragrant bloom of stories past,
In every sigh, their shadows cast.

Unseen hands of fate entwine,
Guiding souls through dusk's design.
With every breath, a life reborn,
In every heart, the love is worn.

To the forgotten, the world still sings,
Of all the beauty that sorrow brings.
In twilight's glow, their spirits rise,
Awakening under starry skies.

Illumination in the Understory

Beneath the canopy, secrets lie,
Where soft leaves whisper, and shadows sigh.
The dance of light through branches weaves,
A tapestry rest where wonder cleaves.

Curled ferns stretch in the gentle breeze,
As nature hums amongst the trees.
Emerald hues in muted tones,
A world alive with vibrant moans.

Soft glimmers, like dreams set free,
Reveal the heart of the forest's plea.
In shadows cast by ancient oak,
Wisdom speaks in the words unspoke.

With each new step, a story blooms,
In hidden paths and fragrant plumes.
The realm of roots, where spirits soar,
In every breath, we seek for more.

The Realm of Shadowed Pines

In twilight's cloak, where silence dwells,
The pines hold secrets, their voices swell.
In shadows deep, where twilight charts,
A world unseen, that tugs at hearts.

Branches cradle the fading light,
Guiding footsteps into night.
The rustle soft beneath our feet,
Nature's hymn, both dark and sweet.

A haunting breeze through boughs does creep,
The ancient woods in silence keep.
Every rustling leaf a sigh,
Echoes of dreams that dare to fly.

In the depths where the shadows play,
A dance of twilight steals the day.
In this realm of forgotten rhymes,
The souls of nature weave their chimes.

Revelations of the Rustic Boughs

Amidst the trees where stories brew,
Boughs bend low with drops of dew.
Whispers float on the morning air,
Revelations hidden, laid bare.

Rough bark cradles time's embrace,
With each ring, a tale of grace.
The rustic scents of earth and pine,
In every breath, a path divine.

With curling tendrils, shadows glide,
As sunlight dances by their side.
Where time stands still, secrets unite,
In the boughs' embrace, shadows bright.

From every leaf, a saga flows,
A tapestry where nature glows.
In every gnarled and twisted way,
The rustic boughs have much to say.